Ponies
"Little 'Equines' With Lots of Heart"
For Kids

Nature Books for Kids
By
K. Bennett

JD-Biz Publishing

Read More Amazing Animal Books

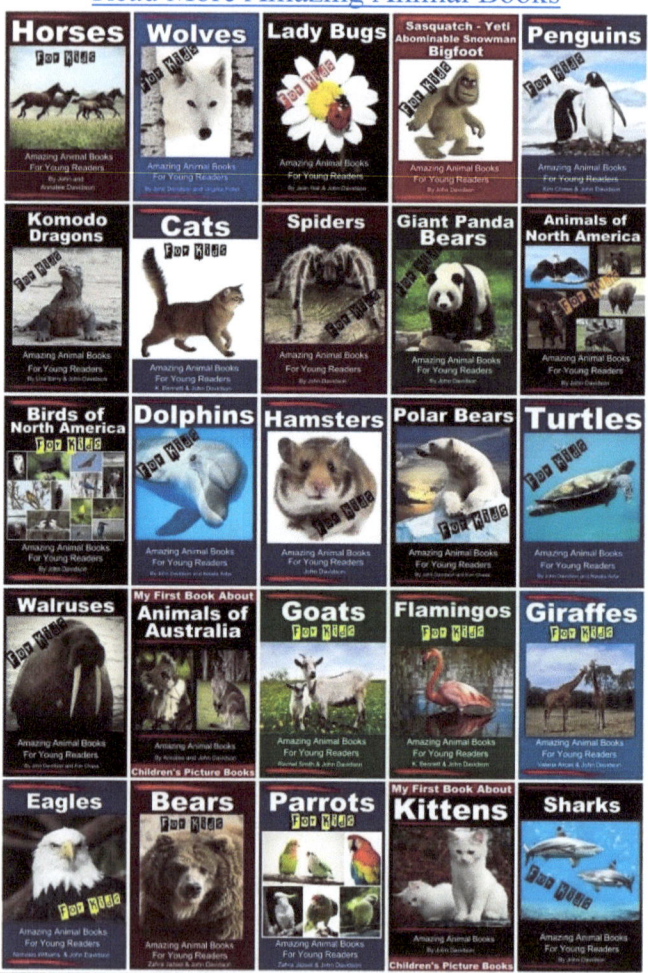

Purchase at Amazon.com

Table of Contents

Introduction

Chapter 1 Great Ponies

Chapter 2 Amazing Creatures

Chapter 3 Pony Fun Facts!

Conclusion Nature's Amazing Wonders

Author Bio

Introduction

*A horse doesn't care how much you know until he knows how much you care ~ **Pat Parelli***

***

Ponies: Ponies are beautiful little equines with big hearts! The name Pony comes from a French word that means: foal. Do you remember what a foal is?

CURIOUS FACT FOR KIDS:

When a horse is born until 6 months of age it's called a *foal*.

But this does not mean a Pony is only a Pony until they are 6 months old! Why? Well, other horses grow up and get different names like: *Yearling, Colt, Stallion, Filly, Gelding and Mare.* But not a Pony. No matter how old a Pony gets, it will still be a Pony!

Ponies are smart and friendly and some of them can be a little hard to handle. But not all of them are like that! Only some. Most Ponies are great for small children to ride, if they are trained in the right way.

Ponies are sometimes called "miniature." Do you know the meaning of this word? Some dictionaries say: "Very small in size." So Ponies are smaller than other horses. You probably know a lot about big horses, so where do Ponies come from?

Sadly, we do not know exactly where Ponies come from, but we do have a good idea. I will tell you more about this in Chapter 1, when we talk about the history of Ponies.

What makes Ponies special?

There are lots and lots of different types of Ponies with lots of coat colors! Here are some of the names:

-American Sport Pony

-American Quarter Pony

-British Riding Pony

-Dartmoor Pony

-Exmoor Pony

-Fell Pony

-Gotland Pony

-Hackney Pony

-Shetland Pony

-Mountain Pony

-New Forest Pony

-Pony of the Americas

-Welara Pony

-Welsh Pony

-Welsh Cob and more!

(Source: *Horses.animal-world.com*)

Ponies in the past

Ponies were used for many things in the past. Things like driving and backing heavy loads. When it came to hauling coal from the mines to help the miners work better, guess who helped? Yes! Ponies did. These types of Ponies were called: *Pit Ponies*. But, don't think it was all bad! Ponies were also used for fun riding and taking small children from one place to another.

Ponies today

Today, Ponies also work in driving and participate in lots of different types of competitions. Ponies are also used in carnivals and private parties for young children. Sometimes you can find them at summer camps, working as pack animals and pulling horse drawn carriages!

Ponies are really amazing little animals. With their beautiful coat colors, fun loving and gentle personality… they are wonderful to learn about. Please take a moment to read a little more about these *"little equines with big hearts!"*

Hello there!

WOULD YOU LIKE TO DRAW A SIMPLE HORSE? LEARN HERE!

Howtodrawanimals.net has a simple 8 step tutorial on drawing horses. I thought you might like to try!

1- **FIRST:** Before you search online, please get a parent's or guardian's permission!

2- In your browser (Chrome, Internet explorer, Firefox, Torch) type: http://www.howtodrawanimals.net/how-to-draw-a-horse

3 – Then follow the steps.

If this tutorial is too difficult for you or if you don't like it, then try the **Wikihow** *tutorial instead:*

1- In your browser (Chrome, Internet explorer, Firefox, Torch) type: www.Wikihow.com

3- In the search box at the top of the page type: *Draw a simple horse*. Once the search is complete, you should see a title that reads: "**How to draw a simple horse: 11 steps with pictures**."

4 – Click on the link and follow the steps.

5- Have fun!

Chapter 1

Hi, just out for a walk with my friend!

History: We don't know that much about the history of Ponies, but we know this…There are lots of different types of Pony breeds! Ponies have a rich ancestry that goes back many, many years. Some people think it goes as far back as the Ice Age Pony! That's a very long time ago, right?

Many people believe Ponies lived in very hard places where it was difficult to survive. They think the ground was rough and there was little food to eat. If you lived in a place like this, do you think you could live or would it be difficult? Well, Ponies did survive and people say this is what makes them strong!

The interesting thing about Ponies is how they get their names. You might be thinking…aren't they all Ponies? That's right! But did you notice the names in the introduction? Before you get to Pony or just after the name, there is always a FIRST or LAST name. For example:

Pony of the Americas. Can you guess where this Pony came from? The Americas? Excellent!

What about ***Dales Pony***? Where did this Pony come from? Yes! Dales. Very good!

And finally, ***Shetland Pony***. Where did this Pony come from? Do you know where Shetland is? It's in the UK, in the northern part of the British Isles. So, where did this Pony come from? Yes! The UK. Outstanding work!

This type of name calling is typical for most Ponies. Usually, they have the name of the region or country where they come from. It is a great way to tell which Pony comes from which place. Neat idea, don't you think?

This does not mean all Ponies are called Ponies! There are Ponies with odd names like:

-Merens

-Icelandic Horse

-Dulmen

-Gotland

-Highland

-Norwegian Fjord

-Prezlwalski's Horse

- Chincoteague pony

It is important to mention that many people fight over these names. Why? Some say they are horses and not Ponies! What do you think? Do some research and come up with your own conclusions.

Remember: Before you search online, please get a parent's or guardian's permission!

After many years and especially during the 20th century, breeders added Arabian horse blood and other types of horses to the Pony breed. Do you remember what **Crossbreeding** is?

The dictionary at Kids.Net.Au defines this word like this: "*(genetics) the act of mixing different species or varieties of animals or plants and thus to produce hybrids.*"

So they mixed the horses together to make new Ponies!

Beautiful coat

Characteristics: What has been the result of this mix-up of horses? Well, Ponies have developed lots of different colors, but they

are still one basic size. How small are they? During competitions Ponies are divided into 3 groups: Small, medium and large.

Small: Approximately 12.2 hands and under

Medium: Approximately 12.2 - 13.2 hands

Large: Approximately 13.2 – 14.2

Miniature Pony Breeds: 34 – 38 inches!

Weight: This can be very different! Ponies can weigh from 200 to 900 pounds. Some Ponies can even weigh a bit more than this and some can weigh a bit less. It all depends on the size!

Coats: Ponies have beautiful coat colors in all shades! They can be black, bay, roan, spotted, brown, pinto and chestnut or even blanket patterns. There are many more colors than these, but it's a great way to get started! Do you remember what *Roan* means?

Roan: Is more than one color. It is a pattern of colors mixed with white. So the horse will have lots of white hairs mixed with their other hairs. You can find this mix-up on the head, lower legs, mane and tail. Sometimes, this color variation is called Silvery. Makes me think of the moonlight. Isn't that beautiful?

So, which color variety do you like? Pick one and tell your parents, classmates or guardian about it… and why you like it!

My coat color is cute and so is my friend!

Measuring horses: What is **HANDS**?

This is a neat way to measure horses. The measurement refers to hands, literal hands! The symbol is usually HH (Hands high). So you would say 15hh, 16hh or 17hh. This means 15 hands, 16 hands and 17 hands. You might be wondering why people measure horses in hands?

Well, many years ago people did not have rulers or measuring sticks like we do today. So they used whatever they had…and they had hands. So horses are measured like this. You can do it too! How?

Think about it like this: One hand is 4 inches.

So if a horse is 15 hands multiply this by 4. (15 x 4) and you will get 60 inches. And if a horse is 16 hands multiply this number by 4. (16 x 4) and you will get 64 inches.

Now that you know how to do it, you can measure other horses for yourself.

Remember: Ponies are smaller than normal horses so when you measure… see how much taller or smaller than you they are! Have fun!

Feels good in the snow!

I can see you!

Events: Ponies are used in many different types of sports. Some of these sports are **Gymkhana** and another is **combined driving**. Let's talk about Gymkhana first. In our book: "*Colonial Spanish for Kids*" book, we wrote about this event, but I will repeat it again for you!

Gymkhana: This event (for ponies and horses) is speed pattern racing and timed games for riders and their horses. This means the horses have to race in a certain way and there is a timer too! So they need to finish on the clock and not be late!

If you have never heard of this word before, not to worry! I think the Native American word is better to understand. They call this type of games "*O-Mok-See*," which means: "games on horseback." This means a horse and rider play games together! This show is for many people to enjoy and the horse and rider get points for good horsemanship.

It is not only for adults. Kids get to participate too! Would you like to try? How much you learn and how fast you go is up to you.

Combined driving: This type of competition has another name too: *Horse driving trials*. What does this include? It has to do with a carriage. You can have one horse or Pony, a team of two or a team of four. What do you prefer? One, two or four?

The games can get a little complicated. Why? Because there are three phases: One is dressage, the other is cross-country marathon and the last one is obstacle cone driving.

The dressage part of the event is also divided into two phases: *Presentation* and *Driven dressage*. This is where a horse and its rider should look great! You have to be clean, nicely dressed and smell good too! There are lots of other steps to this competition but it gives you an idea. I would prefer to ride or play with my Pony just for fun! What about you?

Smell the flowers Primrose!

Pony Clubs are another way to learn lots of fun things about Ponies. What is a Pony Club? This international Organization was made to teach young people about how wonderful Ponies are. This club is in approximately 30 countries around the world, but it started in England. It has about 100,000 members who are 8 – 25 years old.

There are different levels like Beginner, Intermediate and Advanced. Would you like to know why the club was formed? ***Wikipedia.org*** says this…

~To encourage young people to ride and to learn to enjoy all kinds of sport connected with horses and riding.

~To give instruction in riding and horse mastership and to educate Members to look after and to take proper care of their animal.

~To promote the highest ideals of sportsmanship, citizenship and loyalty to create strength of character and self-discipline."

I am having so much fun!

Care: Ponies have an independent spirit, which means they like to do some things on their own. But this does not mean you don't have to care for them. They love a happy, loving environment so here are a few important things to think about:

Food: Pones are easy keepers! This means they are easy to care for. So, when it comes to food… grass (good, healthy grass) is a great way to go. A little grain or even no grain is fine too!

Living: If you keep them inside you have to turnout every day. Do you remember what **turnout** means?

In our "*Canadian Horse for Kids*" book, we explained this: "Your horse needs to get out of the stall every day. It needs to run free! Why? Think about this: Do you want to be stuck in one place every day without moving around? Neither does your horse! This will help to reduce their stress and make them feel happy."

Beautiful coat!

Grooming: It depends on the Pony breed. Some will need their hair cut often to keep them healthy and looking great! Don't forget to check the feet too! Keep those shoes (if it has shoes) clean and trimmed. All of these tips are very important for a healthy, happy horse!

Remember: "Take care of your Pony and it will take care of you!"

I love you mommy!

Chapter 2

The view is nice up here!

Have you learned anything new about Ponies? Wonderful! But there is still a little more we can learn about them. How about training? We will detail the steps for training all horses and then give you additional tips on training Ponies! Ready?

Training: *Wikihow.com* recommends the following steps to train horses:

1-***First of all, don't scare the horse***. That means you should not run up or sneak up on them suddenly. This is not a hard to understand. Do you like it when people run or sneak up on you suddenly? It may scare you when someone does that, right? Then a horse will feel the same way.

2-*Be gentle and talk kindly to your horse*. There is no need to yell, shout or talk in a harsh tone to your horse. Again, this idea is not hard to understand. Do you like it when people talk to you gently? Or do you want them to shout and yell at you? Isn't it nicer to treat others kindly and don't you appreciate it when others do the same for you? Your horse will appreciate your kind manner too!

The flowers smell good!

3-*Most horses love to be touched*. Show them your feelings through your hands. Stroke them on the head, massage their neck, hug them, brush them and communicate your affection through gentle fingers. Imagine how happy your horse will be!

4-*Try to spend as much time as you can with your horse*. In any friendship, regular visits are the key! No matter what you have to do, stop by and visit your horse just to remind them that you're there. They will be so happy to see you and the more you spend time with them, the stronger your bond will grow.

5- *A nice reward*. A tasty treat, rub or pat down, yummy food, grooming of whatever other treat you might have in mind, will be a great idea! Do this at the end of the day to let your horse know how much you enjoyed spending time with them.

This sand is good for my feet!

Ponies training skills: It is good to understand that Ponies can be gentle and sweet, but some may be hard to handle. Why? Well, just like us, they have good days and bad days! And just like us some can be quiet and others can get into trouble! And on the bad days they may be a little stubborn too!

With all of the different types of personalities, what is the best thing to do? Simple! Listen to people who KNOW about the subject. These training experts can help you understand the best way to train your Pony!

April Reeves from *Aprilreeveshorsetraining.wordpress.com* says it best when she writes: *"The horse you lead is the horse you ride."* So, the right training goes a long way to having a nice, responsible horse!

She lists the most important ingredients in training like:

-Consistency

-Timing

-Repetition

-Patience and Calm!

Ponies

You can do it!

HorseandriderUk.com says this:

"Plenty of turns and circles." Why so many turns and circles? Because you want your Pony to listen to you! Every time you change to a turn or a circle, your Pony will learn obedience, which is a good thing!

Another thing he or she will learn is control. WHO is in control and it is NOT him or her! It is you. ***Remember:*** Ponies can be stubborn and hard to handle. But with lots of love, firm kindness and patience you can teach your horse to be great!

Set goals and rewards. This means: If you plan to teach your pony how to stand in one place when you want him to stand in one place…give him a small gift (a nice bite to eat) when he does it! Don't you like to get gifts when you have done something good? Your horse might feel the same way.

With these tips in mind, you will have a happy, confident and loving horse!

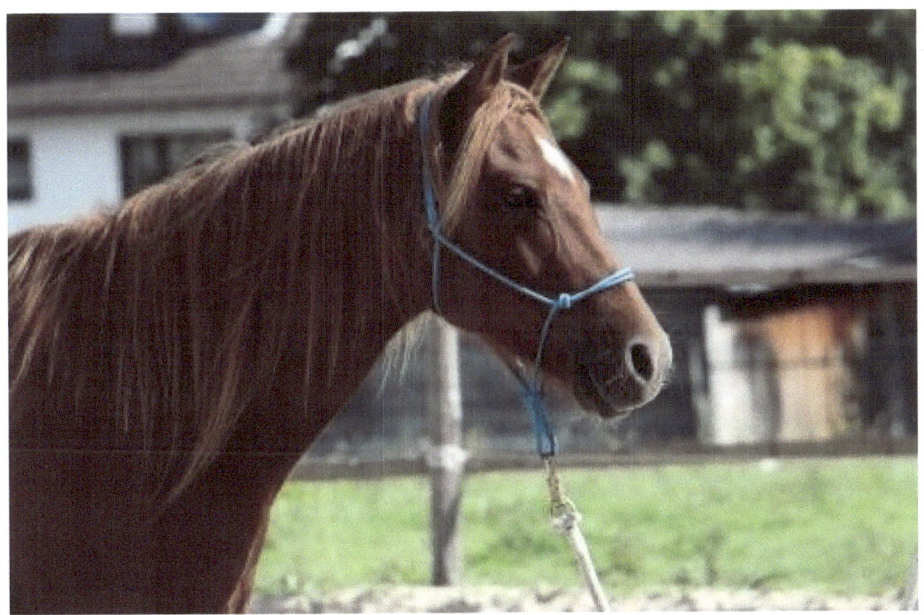

Where is my apple?

Chapter 3

Ponies and horses are the same type of animal called Equines, but they are very different too! How so? Here are four of those differences:

-A typical horse will stand over 14.2 hands. Ponies stand below this number.

-Personality and temperament help to decide between a Pony and a horse. Characteristics are important too. For example, a pony will have a thicker mane, tail and coat. They also have heavier bones than horses.

- Ponies are sometimes easier to get along with and calmer, so children love to ride them! Adults love them too!

I love my Pony!

- Ponies are stronger than horses. Why? Because they are much heavier pound by pound!

Hey! Let's run in the field together!

INTERESTING HORSE FACTS FOR KIDS:

- Horses are great at listening! They can turn their ears in different ways to improve their hearing. If you whisper and say something bad about your horse, they just might hear you!

-Horses are the best sleepers on the planet. They can sleep lying down and standing up! Can you do that?

- Horses are herbivores. Do you know that this means? It means they eat plants or are plant eaters, if you like this term better.

-Horses have feelings and emotions too! Treat them kindly with lots of patience and love. You may be surprised at the results!

-After a horse is born in just a few hours it can run away from you!

-There was a horse that lived many years ago called "Old Billy," also called Billy Boy or Billy. Guess how long he lived? 62 years! Wow, isn't that amazing?

(Source: **Onekind.org & Sciencekids.co.nz**)

Hey there!

Remember: Before you search online, please get a parent's or guardian's permission!

Conclusion:

In conclusion: Horses are beautiful creatures, and Ponies are no different! They are strong, gentle and intelligent equines! And all of them are a wonderful example of how amazing Earth's creatures can be.

This is a great time to learn a bit more about these noble animals. You may like to check out the Ponies Club for more information. Or you may like to read the website: Pony Access (www.ponyaccess.com) which talks about the SAFE way to train ponies to help children with disabilities. This website is very interesting and might make a fun study!

After your research, you may be amazed at what you can discover. There are also multiple free printables online with Ponies and horses.

You might like to check out this site: http://educationalcoloringpages.com/mylittlepony.html

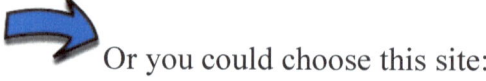Or you could choose this site: http://www.craftyponies.co.uk/kids-activities/4559682842

Here is another choice: http://www.printactivities.com/Theme-Printables/Horse-Printables.html

And one more: http://www.activityvillage.co.uk/horses

If you don't know exactly what to research about Ponies, then think about this: Choose some part of the horse you really like (It can be the tail, mane, ears, body, size, personality, history, etc) and learn a bit more about that subject.

Another option is this: If you are in school and participate in show and tell, use that as your subject. Many of your classmates may not even know what a Pony is really like, so it would be nice to share what you find with others!

I hope you have learned just a little bit about the wonderful world of Ponies, and how they can add diversity to our life in amazing ways!

"Educating the mind without educating the heart is no education at all." - *Aristotle*

Author Bio

K. Bennett loves to write for both children and adults. Many different subjects are interesting to develop, but writing for children is special to her heart.

Her favorite pastimes include reading, traveling and discovering new things. Each of these activities helps to fuel her imagination and acts like a blank canvas waiting for more stories.

She is intrigued with fantasy elements like hidden worlds and faraway lands. Basically anything that gets her imagination soaring to new heights!

Her writing credits include children books online, short stories for online magazines, and two novellas listed at Amazon.com

Our books are available at

1. Amazon.com

2. Barnes and Noble

3. Itunes

4. Kobo

5. Smashwords

6. Google Play Books

Publisher

JD-Biz Corp

P O Box 374

Mendon, Utah 84325

http://www.jd-biz.com/

Ponies

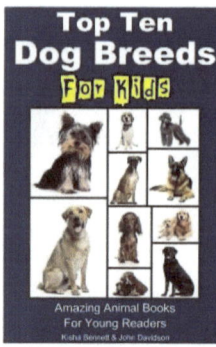

Top Ten Dog Breeds For Kids
Amazing Animal Books For Young Readers
Kisha Bennett & John Davidson

German Shepherds
Dog Books for Kids
K. Bennett

Bulldogs
Dog Books for Kids
K. Bennett

Dachshund
Dog Books for Kids
K. Bennett

Poodles
Dog Books for Kids
K. Bennett

Labrador Retrievers
Dog Books for Kids
K. Bennett

Rottweilers
Dog Books for Kids
K. Bennett

Boxers
Dog Books for Kids
K. Bennett

Golden Retrievers
Dog Books for Kids
K. Bennett

Puppies
Dog Books For Kids
Amazing Animal Books
By John Davidson

Beagles
Dog Books for Kids
K. Bennett

Yorkshire Terriers
Dog Books for Kids
K. Bennett

Dogs
Top Ten Dog Breeds For Kids
Amazing Animal Books For Young Readers
Zahra Jazeer & John Davidson

Cats For Kids
Amazing Animal Books For Young Readers
K. Bennett & John Davidson

Foxes For Kids
Amazing Animal Books For Young Readers
Zahra Jazeel & John Davidson

Wolves For Kids
Amazing Animal Books For Young Readers
By John Davidson and Virginia Fidler

Ponies

Ponies

Ponies

Learn How to Draw and Paint

Horses

For The Beginner

Step By Step Guide to Drawing Horses with Pencil, Charcoal, Pastels, Airbrush Watercolors and Cartoons

Learn To Draw Series

Paolo Lopez de Leon and John Davidson